Cacophony

AF632852

Corinne Rose

BookLeaf Publishing

Presentation by *BookLeaf Publishing*

Web: www.bookleafpub.com

E-mail: info@bookleafpub.com

ISBN: 9789357211147

First edition 2022

DEDICATION

I thought about dedicating this to Ryan and the boys. I thought about dedicating this to my friends. But, in all honesty, this book is dedicated to my mom. My mom, who always bragged about my poetry to anyone that would listen. I finally did it, Mom. This one's for you. To the moon and back. xoxo

ACKNOWLEDGEMENT

Ryan- For not questioning this whim, and fully supporting me through this challenge, and life in general.

ROAR and THOR- For giving me new motivation to be all the things I've always wanted to be.

Azechia- Just for existing. And being the best little brother any big sister could have ever asked for. For your uncanny ability to tell me something I need to hear, even when I don't realize I need it. And just for being you.

Lys and Cassie- Super Salad on me when I sell my first copy.

PREFACE

I don't apologize for the emotional whiplash you may experience while reading this mess.

Dust

When I found it again
It was covered
In a layer of dust

Not the light kind
Like a blanket of spring snow
When winter is fighting to hold on

Not the delicate kind
That you can blow away
Like wish candles on a cake

This was the thick kind
The sticky dust
That covers forgotten knick knacks in the attic

The kind that takes water
And elbow grease
To get out of the nooks and crannies

Shoved back in a dark corner
Unrecognizable
Suffering from decades of neglect

But there it was
And with some love
My poetry came alive once again

A Poem About Cheese

Swiss, Havarti, Provolone
On crackers, bread, or on a scone
Ooey, gooey, warm and runny
A poem about cheese might be funny
Milk from cows, milk from goats
I like cheese with herbal notes
Pizza, pasta, nachos, fries
Even cheddar on apple pies
Grilled cheese sandwich? I'll take three
Cheese pulls are the thing for me
On it's own or as an addition
To eat all the cheese is my mission

Awakening

I wondered if I could even do it
Could I even remember how to rhyme?
It's been so long, I cannot tell
I guess it will take me some time

My rhythm feels like it's off
And even more, my turn of phrase
But this is for awakening
So much more that it's for praise

This was such a part of me
These words, this paper, this pen
I'm sure if I just try enough
It will feel natural again

So I will fight the doubt
The mean things that echo in my head
To bring back life to what's been gone
Like a butterfly when the cocoon is shed

That last stanza felt a little forced
But I will keep it, every line
I wasn't sure if I remembered
But I'm remembering just fine

Throw this haiku in a crockpot.

Salt, pepper, garlic,
Cream cheese, yogurt, parmesan,
Spinach, artichokes

The Ballad of Roar and Thor

My sweet little darlings
You are to blame
You gave me new eyes
To see all the pain
I've carried through life
Without any thought
Because you are here
Maybe I ought
To heal these wounds
And tend to my scars
Learn from mistakes
End curses where they are
We can forge a new path
And write a new story
So when you are grown
I won't have to say sorry
For causing you pain
And making you suffer
Because I didn't know
And you were my buffer
My anger won't fall
Onto your tiny shoulders
I will raise you as humans
And not litte soldiers

Fighting for yourselves
Fighting for each other
I will do this thing right
Because I am your mother
I will be the adult
And you can be children
And you won't even know
But I know I will when
You've grown up strong
And you've grown up happy
This may sound a bit silly
This may sound a bit sappy
But Mommy will heal
And be better for you
And you'll never understand
What Mommy went through
As long as I'm here
I will do what I can
So this is your fault
I hope you understand

Are Haikus Cheating?

If I think too long
Haikus feel like a cop out
But you're getting them

Cacophony

Pen to paper
Mind goes blank
No clever quips
Or even words

Words, words, words
Rhymes and rhymes
A book full of poetry
Twenty-one times

I don't know what to write
How do I know what's right?
Should this one have been left?

This is my cacophony
Of words, some of them rhyme
This is a poetry challenge
I will finish on time

Robert Frost, Is That You?

Light glitters through the trees
An illuminating golden glow
The moss covered ground ahead
Newly emerged from months of snow

The stream babbles happily nearby
Zigging, zagging, to and fro
The ground is full of winter's last
You can hear the squishing as you go

A gentle walk through a springtime wood
At dusk or at dawn
Do you want to see it wake
Or ending the day with a yawn?

Haiku Break In 5 Parts: Part I

A rhyming haiku?
Is that something you can do?
Is it old or new?

Haiku Break In 5 Parts: Part II

Watercolor Paint
Crayons, pencils, markers, pens
Craft time is the best

Haiku Break In 5 Parts: Part III

Ten fingers, Ten toes
Big doe eyes, cute little nose
Squish baby face

Haiku Break In 5 Parts: Part IV

Some more about cheese
If you eat it when you're sad
You will feel happy

Haiku Break In 5 Parts: Part V

If you don't produce
Seratonin-Dopamine
Store bought is just fine

Deep Dark Danger

There are times I get lost
Inside of my head
In the dark hidden places
Where things want me dead
I try to stay out but
That place pulls me in
A black hole in my mind
That begs for my skin
The darkness wans a host
To let it go free
And because it's in my head
That host is me
I try to avoid it
By distracting myself
To lock it away
Hide the key on a shelf
But sometimes I'm curious
Look behind that locked door
And it pulls me right in
I'm not safe anymore
The more that I fight it
The stronger it grows
It's faster than quicksand
I can't get the door closed
Somedays it fings a way

Through some of the cracks
These days are okay
I have a chance to fight back
But the days it takes over
And I spiral down
Are the days I don't know
If I'll ever be found
The darkness is anger
The darkness is grief
The darkness is fear
The darkness, a theif
It steals away joy
It causes me pain
It takes all my strength
Makes me feel ashamed
When it gets its freedom
I don't know who I am
When I lock it away
I still feel so damned
I'm always on guard
It's constantly prying
I'm so tired of fighting
I'm so tired of lying
Saying I'm fine
While fighting this battle
Every single day of my life
That damn door does rattle
I'm going to give in
I'm going to visit

The darkness inside me
I'll ask "What is it?"
If it's simply grief
And anger and pain
And it's locked away
Inside my brain
There's a reason it's here
Isn't that right?
Shouldn't I ask
Instead of just fight?
Not pushing away
And denying it exists
Maybe I'll fing out
Something I've missed
Maybe the darkness
Doesn't want me dead
Maybe it's living
Inside of my head
Because it was always
There to protect me
When those that should have
Would only neglect me
I don't think the darkness
Is something to fear
And I've misunderstood
The reason it's here
I've been through some shit
I can't deny that
And maybe my darkness

Helped me fight back
A primal reaction
To very real threats
When angry and sad
Were as good as it gets
But now that I'm safe
And on stable footing
I'm wasting my energy
That I could be putting
Into something I'm proud of
Something I love
Or anything better
Than a constant push/shove
There's something inside me
Of that there's no doubt
But I'll sit and talk with it
And then let it out
We are safe, we are happy
We're on stable ground

Inside me, you'll never
Guess what I found
I unlocked that door
With that hidden key
The darkness inside
Had always been me
A scared little girl
Curls and a dress
She was simply afraid

And doing her best
To keep us safe
When we were triggered
The more pain we were in
Her fright just grew bigger
After some coaxing
She's finally free
It'll take some adjusting
But now she can just be

By The Gaslight

Gaslight, burning bright
The last thing I hear tonight
You saying I'm crazy and calling me lazy
And I don't even put up a fight

Gaslight, burning brighter
Because I've never been a fighter
I'm isolated and manipulated
My submission is your lighter

Gaslight, burned so bright
But I finally saw the light
I got away and to this day
I'm so glad I learned to fight

An Unapology

This book of poems
Is quite unpolished
I'm rusty
To say the least

It's been a battle
To get this thing done
It feels like
Wrestling a beast

But I've pushed through
And got them all out
Some are forced
Some, a cathartic release

I'm proud of this book
And this rusty poetry
It's been some time
SInce I've felt this peace

More About Cheese (Another Haiku)

Have you ever had
Cheddar so aged it's crunchy?
Yummy, crunchy cheese

This Is Actually A Recipe

First you take the noodles
And you rinse them well
Grate at least two pounds of cheese
The type is for your heart to tell

Cube up two blocks of cream cheese
Set all your ingredients to the side
Get your crockpot greased or lined
Here comes a preparation guide

Layer noodles and layer cheese
Until everything is all used up
Crock it til your noodles cook
Stir in milk, about a cup

Salt, pepper, garlic, nutmeg
Any seasonings you would like
Crockpot macaroni and cheese
That'll make you drop the mic

www.ingramcontent.com/pod-product-compliance
Lightning Source LLC
Chambersburg PA
CBHW051756130826
49812CB00033B/1177
9789357211147